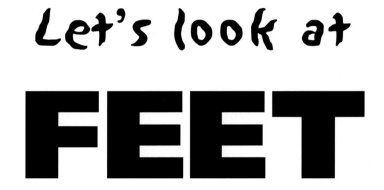

Let's look at
FEET

First published in 2001 by Zero To Ten Limited
327 High Street, Slough, Berkshire, SL1 1TX
This edition published under license from Zero To Ten Limited. All rights reserved.

Copyright © 2001 Zero To Ten Limited
Text copyright © 2001 Simona Sideri
Illustrations copyright © 2001 Sheilagh Noble

Publisher: Anna McQuinn, Art director: Tim Foster, Publishing assistant: Vikram Parashar

Published in the United States by Smart Apple Media
1980 Lookout Drive, North Mankato, Minnesota 56003

U.S. publication copyright © 2005 Smart Apple Media
International copyright reserved in all countries. No part of this book may be reproduced in
any form without written permission from the publisher.
Printed in China

Library of Congress Cataloging-in-Publication Data

Sideri, Simona.
Feet / written by Simona Sideri ; illustrated by Sheilagh Noble.
p. cm. — (Let's look at)
Summary: Children introduce the variety of feet found in the animal kingdom
and describe how they are used.
ISBN 1-58340-492-9
1. Foot—Juvenile literature. [1. Foot. 2. Animals. 3. Anatomy.] I. Title: Let's look
at feet. II. Noble, Sheilagh, ill. III. Title. IV. Let's look at (North Mankato, Minn.)

QM549.S544 2004
571.3'1—dc22   2003058960

9 8 7 6 5 4 3 2 1

Let's look at
FEET

Written by
Simona Sideri

Illustrated by
Sheilagh Noble

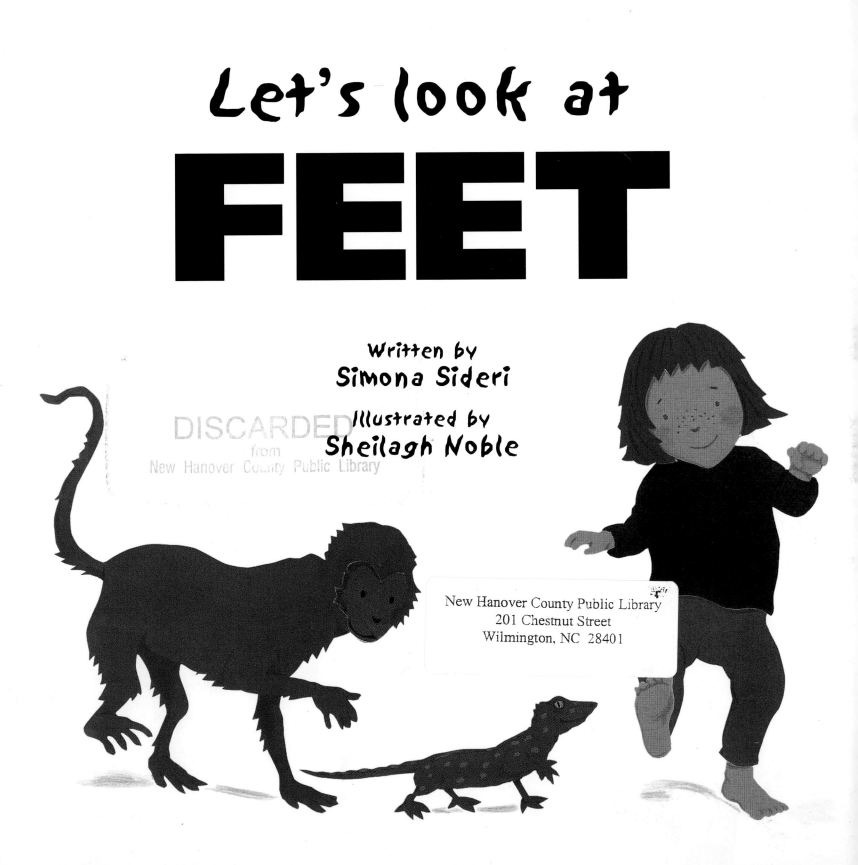

Feet are fantastic!

How many toes are on each?

An elephant has five toes, too.

But elephants' feet
are much bigger
than ours.

Horses have hard hooves.

They are great for galloping!

A camel's hooves are special.

They have
two toes
that spread
out flat
so the camel
doesn't sink
in soft sand.

Birds' claws
are special!

They curl around branches and hold on tight.

A duck-billed platypus
   has webbed feet
      to help it swim swiftly...

and dive deep.

Geckos
can hang
upside-down...

to catch the insects they eat.

They have sticky pads on their feet.

Feet are **fantastic!**

Some are fast and some are fancy...

But mine are best for me!